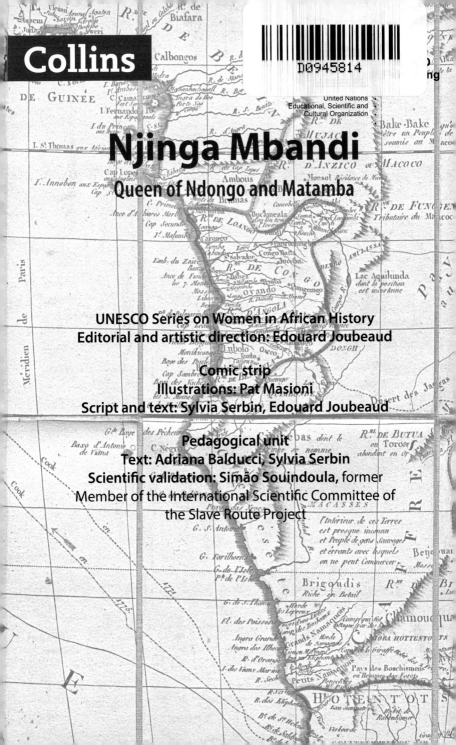

**Collins**

United Nations
Educational, Scientific and
Cultural Organization

# Njinga Mbandi

## Queen of Ndongo and Matamba

UNESCO Series on Women in African History
Editorial and artistic direction: Edouard Joubeaud

Comic strip
Illustrations: Pat Masioni
Script and text: Sylvia Serbin, Edouard Joubeaud

Pedagogical unit
Text: Adriana Balducci, Sylvia Serbin
Scientific validation: Simão Souindoula, former
Member of the International Scientific Committee of
the Slave Route Project

# UNESCO
# Publishing

United Nations
Educational, Scientific and
Cultural Organization

Published jointly by the United Nations Educational, Scientific and Cultural Organization (UNESCO), 7, place de Fontenoy, 75352 Paris 07 SP, France and HarperCollins Publishers Ltd, Westerhill Road, Bishopbriggs, Glasgow G64 2QT, United Kingdom

First published in this format 2015
© UNESCO 2015
Collins® is a registered trademark of HarperCollins Publishers

ISBN (HarperCollins) 978-0-00-814937-6
ISBN (UNESCO) 978-92-3-100114-7

10 9 8 7 6 5 4 3 2 1

Published in 2014 by the United Nations Educational, Scientific and Cultural Organization
7, place de Fontenoy, 75352 Paris 07 SP, France
© UNESCO 2014

The designations employed and the presentation of material throughout this publication do not imply the expression of any opinion whatsoever on the part of UNESCO concerning the legal status of any country, territory, city or area or of its authorities, or concerning the delimitation of its frontiers or boundaries.

The ideas and opinions expressed in this publication are those of the authors; they are not necessarily those of UNESCO and do not commit the Organization.

The UNESCO Series on Women in African History, produced by the Knowledge Societies Divisions of UNESCO's Communication and Information Sector, was conducted in the framework of the Priority Africa Intersectoral Platform and the General History of Africa Project, in partnership with the History and Memory for Dialogue Section, with the support of the Division for Gender Equality. This initiative was realized with the financial contribution of the Republic of Bulgaria.

UNESCO specialist responsible for the project: Sasha Rubel
Editorial and artistic direction: Edouard Joubeaud

Printed and bound in Hong Kong

# Contents

# Introduction

## Spotlight on women!

The UNESCO Women in African History Series, and its corresponding website, aims to highlight a selection of key women figures in African history.

Through the use of Information and Communication Technology (ICT), the project showcases 20 African women or women of African descent. It demonstrates that, historically, women have distinguished themselves in diverse fields such as politics (Gisèle Rabesahala), diplomacy and resistance against colonization (Njinga Mbandi), defence of women's rights (Funmilayo Ransome-Kuti) and environmental protection (Wangari Maathai).

This list of 20 women represents only a small part of the contribution of African women, known and unknown, to the history of their countries, Africa and all mankind.

Photographs: Huda Shaarawy, around 1900 *(l)*. Unknown photographer; Wangari Mathaii *(c)*. Martin Rowe/The Green Belt Movement, CC-BY-NC-SA 2.2; Sojourner Truth *(r)*, around 1870. © UNESCO/Randall Studio.

Through this project and by emphasizing the education, academic careers and main achievements of these exceptional women, UNESCO seeks to highlight their legacy and calls for continued research on the role of women in African history.

*Visit and share the UNESCO website on Women Figures in African History:*

**www.unesco.org/womeninafrica**

Photographs: Statue of Yennega, Burkina Faso *(l)*. © UNESCO/Brenda Gael McSweeney, 2009; Funmilayo Ransome-Kuti in 1970 *(c)*. © UNESCO/Ransome-Kuti family; Statue of Njinga Mbandi in Luanda, Angola *(r)*. © UNESCO/Erik Cleves Kristensen, 2006, CC-BY 2.0.

# Gender equality: a global priority of UNESCO

The Organization strives to promote gender equality and women's empowerment by integrating these principles in all its programmes, notably in education.

Education makes possible the transmission of the essential value of gender equality: it provides leverage to enforce the fundamental human rights of women and highlights their central role in all societies.

As such, the teaching of history has a crucial role to play since it enables the understanding of cultural features, and highlights the social, political, and economic conditions in the lives of women in past societies.

Hery Zo Rakotondramanana, CC-BY-SA 2.0.

# The General History of Africa

This publication is part of UNESCO's *General History of Africa project*.

Phase I of the project was launched in 1964 and completed in 1999. It resulted in the preparation and publication of a collection of eight volumes, a main edition, and an abridged version which have been translated into thirteen languages (including three African languages). A digital version available for download can be found on the UNESCO website.

Phase II, launched in 2009 and entitled *The Pedagogical Use of the General History of Africa*, aims to develop educational content in order to encourage the teaching of African history. The Women in African History project has been developed within the framework of Phase II.

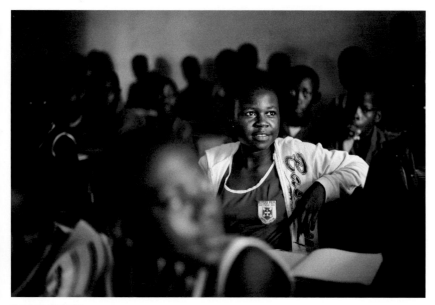

Ben Grey, CC-BY 2.0.

# Biography

## Njinga Mbandi, Queen of Ndongo and Matamba

Njinga Mbandi (1581–1663), Queen of Ndongo and Matamba, defined much of the history of seventeenth-century Angola. The Europeans' mercantilist designs, in particular the development of the slave trade along the southern African coast, drastically changed the political, social, economic and cultural environment of the Kingdom of Ndongo and the entire region. It was against that backdrop that Njinga Mbandi made her mark as an outstanding example of female governance.

Ngola Mbandi Kiluanji, the King of Ndongo, died in 1617. His son, Ngola Mbandi, became the new king but he had neither his father's charisma nor the intelligence of his sister Njinga Mbandi. In 1622,

Statue of Njinga Mbandi, Luanda, Republic of Angola.

harried by the Portuguese, he sent Njinga Mbandi to Luanda as his envoy to negotiate for peace with Dom João Correia de Sousa, the Portuguese Governor. Njinga proved to be an outstanding negotiator and diplomat.

In 1624, Ngola Mbandi died. Njinga took power and became queen. She quickly distinguished herself as an excellent sovereign. Her tactics in warfare and espionage, her diplomatic skills, her ability to forge numerous strategic alliances, and her knowledge of trade and religious issues served her well in tenaciously resisting Portugal's colonialist aspirations until her death in 1663.

# Timeline 1443 – 1623

The Regent, D. Pedro, issues a decree proclaiming a Portuguese monopoly on navigation along the West African coast.

The Portuguese navigator Paulo Dias de Novais arrives in the Kingdom of Ndongo.

Outbreak o[f] war betwee[n] Ndongo and t[he] Portuguese

| 1443 | 1455 | 1560 | 1575 | c. 1580 |

The *Romanus Pontiflex* papal bull by Pope Nicholas V confirms that the Kingdom of Portugal has dominion over lands to the south of Cape Boujdour and Cape Chaunar.

Paulo Dias de Novais founds the city of Luanda.

Ngola Mbandi Kiluanji, the father of Njinga Mbandi, becomes King of Ndongo.

Njinga travels to Luanda as Ndongo's envoy to negotiate a peace treaty with the Portuguese Governor, Dom João Correia de Sousa.

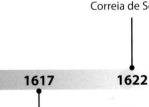

| 1581/82 | 1592 | 1617 | 1622 | 1623 |

Birth of Njinga Mbandi.

Death of Ngola Mbandi Kiluanji. Ngola Mbandi, Njinga Mbandi's brother, becomes king.

Christening of Njinga Mbandi as Dona Ana de Sousa in Luanda.

# Timeline 1623 – 1975

Njinga becomes Queen of Ndongo on her brother's death.

Establishment of the new capital of Njinga's kingdom in Matamba.

Battle of Seng at Kavangaer Njinga's arm combats 20,0 Portuguese soldiers.

**1623/24**     **1626-1629**     **1630/31**     **1641-1648**     **1646**

Njinga loses her throne and retreats to Matamba.

Njinga forges a strategic alliance with the Dutch, who occupy Luanda at the time.

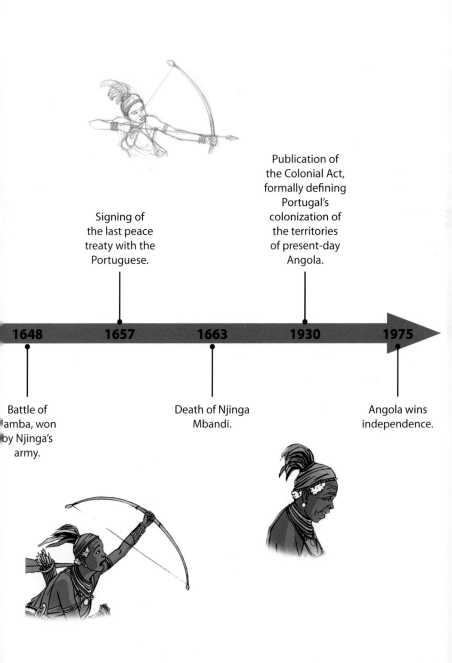

Publication of the Colonial Act, formally defining Portugal's colonization of the territories of present-day Angola.

Signing of the last peace treaty with the Portuguese.

| 1648 | 1657 | 1663 | 1930 | 1975 |

Battle of
amba, won
by Njinga's
army.

Death of Njinga
Mbandi.

Angola wins
independence.

# Comic strip

## Njinga Mbandi, Queen of Ndongo and Matamba

### Foreword

The following comic strip is an interpretation of certain periods in the life of Njinga Mbandi. The illustrations are based on historical and iconographic research on Njinga Mbandi and the seventeenth century in Angola. They do not claim to be an exact representation of the events, people, architecture, hairstyles, or clothing of the period.

A key figure in African resistance to colonialism, Queen Njinga defined much of the history of seventeenth-century Angola. An outstanding strategist and skilful negotiator, she defended her country steadfastly until her death in 1663 at the age of 82.

It was the sixteenth century.
The Kingdom of Ndongo was under threat.

Maritime exploration, initiated by Europeans in the fifteenth century in a bid to conquer new lands, brought the Portuguese to southwest Africa, and the region of present-day Angola.

In 1560, after a long voyage, the Portuguese explorer Paulo Dias de Novais landed on the Ndongo coast, close to the mouth of the Kwanza River.

Paulo Dias de Novais, accompanied by Portuguese Jesuits, traders and dignitaries, announced that he had been sent by the Portuguese Crown and requested to be presented to the King of Ndongo.

When the visitors arrived in Kabasa, capital of Ndongo, they were brought before Ngola Kiluanje kia Ndambi, Njinga's great-grandfather and the King of Ndongo. The King was not deceived by the presents sent by the Portuguese Crown and reacted coldly.

During their stay, the Portuguese learnt that the society was hierarchical and well organized and that Ndongo's inhabitants had many skills in areas such as trade, metalworking, animal husbandry and agriculture.

They took stock of the country's wealth and, in particular, looked for gold and silver mines, much coveted by the Portuguese Crown for its mint.

Five years later, Ngola Kiluanje kia Ndambi authorized Paulo Dias de Novais to leave for Portugal, on the condition that he returned at the head of an army, to help the Ngola to fight against neighbouring kingdoms.

Ten years later, in 1575, Paulo Dias de Novais returned to Ndongo at the head of a fleet of caravels filled with soldiers. His mission was not, however, to help the King of Ndongo, but to seize the country by force, in the name of the King of Portugal.

Ndongo's inhabitants were caught unaware. They defended their homeland valiantly but were beaten back by the Portuguese firepower. Desperation descended on the country.

With lightning speed, the Portuguese seized the Ndongo coastal strip and renamed it Angola. The same year, 1575, they founded the port city of São Paulo da Assunção de Loanda (Luanda). The invasion continued. Ndongo's borders were reduced towards the east, while Portuguese migrants, namely missionaries, farmers and merchants, poured into Luanda, and other adventurers acquired land taken from Africans.

As they found no gold or silver mines, the Portuguese decided to trade in slaves on a massive scale in order to supply labour for the new colony of Brazil.

*They wanted to make Luanda one of the continent's biggest slave-trading ports. They therefore aimed to control the Kwanza River and travel deep into Ndongo territory in order to keep Luanda supplied with slaves.*

It was during these dark times that the young Njinga lived. As she grew up, she saw the resistance put up by her father, King Mbandi Ngola Kiluanji, and the violent changes imposed throughout the region by the Portuguese.

Very early on, Njinga's father discerned in his daughter the fiery temperament and proud intelligence that are the hallmarks of heroes.
On many occasions, she fought at his side against the Portuguese conquistadors and rival kingdoms in the region.

Njinga had been given a good education and been taught to write by visiting Portuguese missionaries and merchants. However, she would never allow her kingdom to be subjugated by a foreign power.

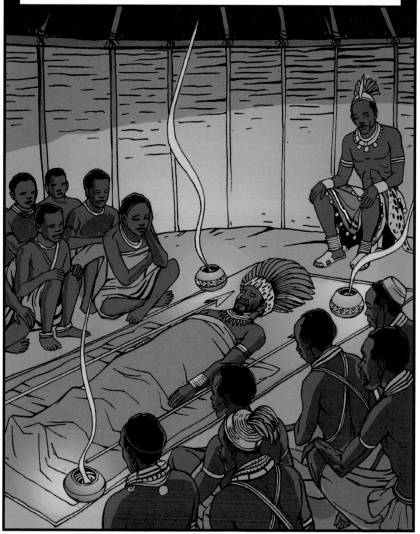

Mbandi Ngola Kiluanji, the King of Ndongo, died in 1617. His son, Ngola Mbandi, took power and became the new king, but he possessed neither his father's charisma nor the intelligence of his sister, Njinga, for whom he felt only hatred and jealousy.

Fearing a plot against him by her entourage, Ngola Mbandi ordered the execution of Njinga's only son, a mere child. Njinga was grief-stricken.

Ngola Mbandi again declared war on the Portuguese but could not repel the enemy's attacks.

The Portuguese, determined to weaken Ndongo at all costs, joined forces with the fearsome Mbangalas, marauding bands of ruthless warriors who ransacked villages and wiped out the inhabitants of the land.

Njinga, deeply troubled by the situation, gathered news from her spies.

Ngola Mbandi finally accepted the elders' advice and instructed Njinga to go to Luanda to negotiate for peace with Dom João Correia de Sousa, the Portuguese Governor.

Luanda! Njinga saw the colonial trading post for the first time.

There were many buildings in the old African village and many more inhabitants than in the past – whites, blacks as well as a new population of mixed origin people.

A little further on, Njinga was stupefied to find an enormous slave shed: before her very eyes, convoys of slaves were being sold and herded on to slave ships. In only a few years, Luanda had become one of the biggest slave-trading ports on the African continent.

Shortly after she arrived, the Portuguese welcomed Njinga graciously and placed a residence at her disposal.

Just before the negotiations, Njinga stood to one side, thinking of the men, women and children on board the slave ships. Where were they going? What did fate have in store for them? She also thought sadly of her son, murdered by her brother a few years before.

The time for negotiations had come, but when Njinga arrived at the palace, she was astounded to find that she was to sit on a carpet spread out before her in the reception room, while the Governor sat in a spacious armchair.

Njinga communicated her wishes to her maid with a mere look: the maid immediately crouched on all fours in front of her so that Njinga could sit on her back.

With that eminently regal gesture, Njinga suggested to the Governor that she had not come to swear allegiance to him, but to negotiate on an equal footing. The negotiations then began.

Njinga reached a twofold agreement: the withdrawal of Portuguese troops from Ndongo and recognition of its sovereignty. In return, she agreed to open trade routes to the Portuguese.

At the Governor's invitation, she extended her stay in Luanda and was introduced to colonial high society. After a few months, she even agreed to be christened as Dona Ana de Sousa, hoping in this way to promote diplomatic relations between Ndongo and Portugal. She was then 40 years old.

Despite regular correspondence between Njinga and the Portuguese Governor, the peace was short-lived. The Viceroy was replaced by a governor who scorned on his predecessor's promises. The Portuguese resumed their onslaught on Ndongo, which was obliged to respond in kind.

In 1624, Njinga's brother, Ngola Mbandi, harried by the Portuguese and the fearsome Mbangalas, retreated to a small island on the Kwanza River, where he died in mysterious circumstances. Did he commit suicide? Did Njinga poison him to avenge her son's murder? Whatever the facts, Njinga, then 43 years of age, took power as Queen of Ndongo and became Ngola Mbandi Njinga Bandi kia Ngola.

She asserted her authority over the local chieftains, conquered the neighbouring Kingdom of Matamba and staunchly defended her two kingdoms.

During the four decades of her rule, the Queen of Ndongo and Matamba vigorously opposed Portugal's colonial designs, building strategic alliances, maintaining a diplomatic correspondence and often directing military operations in person.

One after another, the Portuguese governors came up against this great queen, who unfailingly thwarted their plans. The newly arrived Salvador Correia realized that he could do nothing against this very highly renowned sovereign, then more than 70 years of age.

Finally, the Portuguese Crown renounced its claims to Ndongo in a treaty ratified in Lisbon by King Pedro VI on 24 November 1657.

Queen Njinga died on 17 December 1663 at the age of 82. Throughout her life she valiantly, resolutely and tactically never bowed to adversity. She made her mark as an outstanding sovereign of Ndongo and Matamba, fiercely withstanding colonial designs on the region. She is now considered an eminent historical figure in Angola, Brazil, and many other countries.

# Pedagogical unit contents

## Historical background:
## the Portuguese in Ndongo and resistance

- Local kingdoms
- Slave trade
- Ndongo cornered by the Portuguese

Slaves being loaded onto a European slaving ship.
© UNESCO Illustration from the UNESCO General History of Africa.

# Resistance

- Emergence of a regional political figure
- Outstanding governance by a woman
- A cultivated woman of letters
- An outstanding strategist and diplomat
- A role model for women

The resistance of the African kingdoms against the Europeans.
© UNESCO Illustration from the UNESCO General History of Africa.

# Njinga, an inexhaustible source of inspiration

- Plural and symbolic identities
- Njinga in the arts in past centuries
- Njinga in the arts today
- Religious portrayals in communities of people of African descent

Illustration extracted from the book *Njinga, Reine d'Angola. La Relation d'Antonio Cavazzi de Montecuccolo* presenting the negotiation between Njinga Mbandi and the vice-King of Portugal in Luanda, in 1622.

# Njinga beyond national borders

- A figure closely linked to Angolan identity
- A Pan-African symbol
- A reference in societies where there are people of African descent

Statue of Njinga Mbandi, Luanda, Republic of Angola.

Portrait of Njinga Mbandi by the French illustrator Achille Devéria, 1830.

# Historical background: the Portuguese in Ndongo and resistance

## Introduction

The arrival of the Portuguese in Ndongo in the late sixteenth century profoundly disrupted the local situation. The wars of conquest, the development of the slave trade and the emergence of new economic markets transformed the political, social, economic and cultural landscape of the region.

It was against a backdrop of resistance that Njinga Mbandi became renowned as an outstanding example of female governance in the history of Africa.

View of Lisbon and Tagus River in the 16th century. Caravel and carrack sailing ships during the age of Portuguese discoveries.
Franz Hogenberg & Georg Braun.

# Local kingdoms

In the sixteenth century, central Africa consisted of different kingdoms, above all the great Kingdom of Kongo, but there were also smaller kingdoms such as Ndongo and Matamba, over which the Kingdom of Kongo slowly lost influence.

At the time, it was relatively common for these political entities to be organized along political and geographic lines, based on centralized power and intermediate tiers known – in Ndongo, for instance – as chieftains (*sobas*).

Owing to trade among the kingdoms, complementary products moved primarily between coastal and inland areas. Those commodities were, in particular, iron, ivory, fabrics, salt and foodstuffs such as fish, animals, and other farm produce.

In Ndongo, centralized power was traditionally passed on by lineage and situated in the interior, at the crossing of trade routes, in order to ensure widespread control.

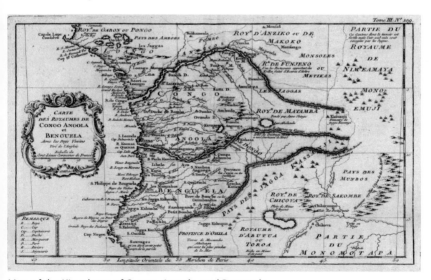

Map of the Kingdoms of Congo, Angola, and Benguela.
© UNESCO/David Rumsey Map Collection.

# Slave trade

From the beginning of the fifteenth century, the Portuguese and the Spanish launched major expeditions to conquer new lands, thus extending their political influence and developing trade links. The Dutch, French and English followed suit one century later.

Portugal's mercantilist venture, especially its large-scale slave-trading operations in Luanda, had a great impact on the local peoples and kingdoms from the late sixteenth century onwards.

In Angola, the slave trade continued until the middle of the nineteenth century. Millions of children, women and men, who had either been rounded up or were victims of wars, raids or local trading, were shipped to Brazil, Central America and Portugal. In addition, Portugal's determination to extend its control over the country gave rise to conflicts, resistance and the interplay of political alliances, either between the invaders and local rulers, or among various local rulers themselves.

Slaves being loaded onto a European slaving ship.
© UNESCO Illustration from the UNESCO General History of Africa.

# Ndongo cornered by the Portuguese

In 1575, the Portuguese navigator and conqueror Paulo Dias de Novais founded the port city of São Paulo da Assunção de Loanda, now the city of Luanda. From 1580 onwards, the Portuguese stepped up their slave-trading activities, declared war on Ndongo and sought to conquer the whole country.

They advanced by stages into the interior, from forts built along the Kwanza River. The construction of Fort Ambaca (1611) took them close to Kabasa, the capital of Ndongo, situated some 250 kilometres from the coast. Decade after decade, successive sovereigns of Ndongo resisted their advance, but were eventually forced to yield before the firepower of the Portuguese and the diplomatic manoeuvres of the Portuguese Crown.

**Successive sovereigns of Ndongo from 1575 to 1663:**

- Njinga Ngola Kilombo kia Kasenda (1575–1592)

- Ngola Mbandi Kiluanji (1592–1617)

- Ngola Mbandi (1617–1623)

- Njinga Mbandi (1623–1663)

The Kwanza River and the church *Nossa Senhora da Conceição*, built by the Portuguese at the end of the sixteenth century.
Paulo Cesar Santos, 2009, CC-BY 1.0

# Resistance

## Introduction

Ndongo's resistance, epitomized by Njinga Mbandi in particular, slowed down Portuguese plans. The Queen relied not only on her skills in warfare, guerrilla methods and her tactics in the field of espionage, but also on her tremendous ability as a negotiator.

Sent to Luanda as an envoy by her brother Ngola Mbandi in 1622, Njinga succeeded in negotiating peace with the Portuguese governor. After her brother's death, Njinga became Queen and tenaciously resisted the Portuguese until her death in 1663.

In spite of numerous attempts to capture her, Njinga thwarted every plot. After her death, the Portuguese occupation was extended deep into the interior of the continent in order to supply slaves to the slave-trading posts, with 7,000 soldiers from Njinga's army being shipped to Brazil as slaves.

The resistance of the African kingdoms against the Europeans.
© UNESCO Illustration from the UNESCO General History of Africa.

# Emergence of a regional political figure

For several decades, Njinga forged many strategic alliances with the neighbouring kingdoms (Kongo, Kassanje and Kissama), negotiated with the Portuguese and the Dutch, and protected people who had taken refuge in her kingdom. She asserted her authority over entire peoples in some instances. She emerged gradually as a powerful political figure in the region and a force to be reckoned with, often feared and never subdued.

Njinga therefore never accepted the loss of Ndongo. Even after fleeing to Matamba, which she had seized, she signed her correspondence with the title Njinga Mbandi Ngola, in other words, Queen of Ndongo and Matamba. As she considered herself to be queen of both kingdoms, she was also known as the "double Queen".

By authorizing the slave trade between the Kingdom of Matamba and Luanda, she allowed a variety of commercial goods to flow between the two regions (domestic animals, fish, textile fibres, palm oil and palm wine), thus contributing to the formation of *kitandas*, popular markets of economic and social importance in which women played a key role.

A *Zungueira* (an Angolan hawker), Luanda, Republic of Angola.
Gilson Oliveira, CC-BY 2.2.

# Outstanding governance by a woman

Njinga played a decisive role in the history of her country and was the catalyst of a genuinely socio-political and cultural revolution. As such, she has been a source of inspiration for African women for hundreds of years.

She is known throughout Africa for her intelligence, her political and diplomatic wisdom, and her flair as a military tactician – and as an exceptional woman and a key historical figure.

# A cultivated woman of letters

Queen Njinga was an educated, cultivated woman. She spoke her native language as well as the language of the Portuguese with whom she had to deal. She wrote her own letters to the Portuguese kings João IV and Alfonso VI and to their governors in Luanda.

Her education, intelligence and command of languages were key assets throughout her life, enabling her to adapt to the most complicated political situations and to turn them to her own advantage. Besides knowing the peoples with whom she was obliged to negotiate, she knew the Portuguese's culture and language, owing to contact in her childhood with the first missionaries and merchants to visit Ndongo.

# An outstanding strategist and diplomat

A dexterous diplomat, she negotiated with the Dutch and the Portuguese to preserve her kingdom's territorial integrity.

Demonstrating extraordinary talent as a strategist, she sent spies regularly to Luanda in order to thwart colonial projects. Their particular mission was to wait for reinforcements to arrive from Lisbon and to study the training methods used by the conquistadors. Njinga thus familiarized her army with Portuguese fighting techniques.

As she preferred guerrilla tactics, her army attacked at night to catch the enemy unaware. In thirty years of warfare, she evaded all traps laid to capture her.

Furthermore, she had a perfect grasp of religious and trade issues. She often used the promise that the Ndongo peoples would convert to Christianity as a bargaining method with the Portuguese. She herself agreed to be christened during a visit to Luanda in 1623.

# A role model for women

Her deeds and strength of character inspired great resistance leaders of the People's Movement for the Liberation of Angola (MPLA) throughout the struggle for independence, in particular: Deolinda Rodrigues, Irene Engracia, Vastok Inga, Mambo Café, Roth Gil and Rita Tomas.

Njinga is a leadership role model for all generations of Angolan women. Women in Angola today display remarkable social independence and are found in the country's army, police force, government, and public and private economic sectors.

# Njinga, an inexhaustible source of inspiration

## Introduction

Since her outmanoeuvring of the Governor, João Correia de Sousa, during the 1622 peace-treaty negotiations in Luanda, the "double Queen" has been acknowledged as an enduring source of inspiration.

Her charisma and the complexity of her personality unfailingly fascinated the missionaries with whom she came into contact, but have also fascinated authors in Europe, Africa and Brazil and, more generally, artists in all countries. Moreover, Njinga has inspired the religious rites of people of African descent throughout the world.

Portrait of Njinga Mbandi by the French illustrator Achille Devéria, 1830.

# Plural and symbolic identities

Njinga's name is written in a variety of ways, partly on account of orthographic issues arising from the transcription of the Kimbundu language, but also because the Queen herself used different names to sign her letters. Among the following names (a non-exhaustive list), the last were given to her when she converted to Catholicism in Luanda in 1623: Njinga Mbande, Njinga Mbandi, Nzinga, Jinga, Singa, Zhinga, Ginga, Njingha, Ana Njinga, Ngola Njinga, Njinga of Matamba, Zinga, Zingua, Mbande Ana Njinga, Ann Njinga and Dona Ana de Sousa.

In Portuguese, the verb *gingar* denotes a movement of the body. Used figuratively, the verb conveys the idea of flexibility in the face of obstacles, especially during negotiations, in reference to Queen Njinga.

# Njinga in the arts in past centuries

In 1687, in a book dedicated to the "double Queen", the Italian priest Cavazzi described the famous 1622 meeting in Luanda between Njinga and Correia de Sousa, the Portuguese Governor, at which a peace treaty was negotiated. When the Queen arrived in the reception room, the governor did not offer her a chair on which to sit. Stung by this action, she ordered one of her servants to crouch on all fours to make a seat for her, thus subtly suggesting that she had come to negotiate on an equal footing. This act inspired the priest Cavazzi to capture the scene in a now famous painting.

Illustration extracted from the book *Zingha, Reine d'Angola. La Relation d'Antonio Cavazzi de Montecuccolo* presenting the negotiation between Njinga Mbandi and the vice-King of Portugal in Luanda, in 1622.

In 1769, the French author Jean-Louis Castilhon published *Zingha, Reine d'Angola* [Njinga, Queen of Angola], the first historical novel to be written on Africa from an anti-colonialist standpoint. The novel, depicting the queen as a rich, paradoxical and complex character, caused quite a stir.

In 1830, Achille Devéria, the French illustrator, fired by enthusiasm after reading portrayals of the Queen of Ndongo and Matamba, decided to draw her portrait. His imaginary depiction of Njinga was widely accepted in Europe as the official portrait of Queen Njinga.

# Njinga in the arts today

Njinga has inspired many authors and artists in recent times. The following are but a few examples:

In 1960, Agostinho Neto wrote the poem *O Içar da Bandeira* [Raising the Banner] in tribute to the Angolan people's heroes, with reference to Njinga.

In 1975, Manuel Pedro Pacavira published the novel *Njinga Mbandi*.

Njinga also inspired the eponymous film made in 2007 by Octávio Bezerra, the Brazilian film director.

In Brazil, a tribute was paid to the Queen at the 2010 Carnival in Rio de Janeiro, based on Alberto Mussa's novel *O Trono da Rainha Ginga* [Queen Ginga's Throne].

Poster of the film *Nzinga* directed by the Brazilian director Octávio Bezerra, 2007.

# Religious portrayals in communities of people of African descent

Njinga has inspired many religions of African origin. In Haiti, in a variant of voodoo, Njinga is symbolized as a Bantu-Ewe-Fon character.

In Brazil, she is portrayed in *Candomblé* (an Afro-Brazilian religion) as the character 'Matamba' – the Lady of Thunder, a warrior chieftain and a friend of the heroes. Women seeking the strength to solve their problems ritually invoke her.

Njinga also features in the Brazilian tradition of *Congada*, a religious rite that blends African traditions and European culture, performed in homage to black saints. In this rite, the coronation of the King of Kongo and Queen Njinga symbolize the advent of Christianity in Angola and Brazil.

The figure of Matamba in *Candomblé*.
© UNESCO/Ana Alves, 2012.

# Njinga Mbandi beyond national borders

## Introduction

In 2013, at the request of the Republic of Angola, UNESCO marks the 350th anniversary of the death of Njinga, a key figure in African history. The celebrations highlight the importance of her influence in Angola, Africa and Europe, and in many societies where there are people of African descent.

## A figure closely linked to Angolan identity

Through her travels in the region, her ability to create alliances, and her unification of peoples, Njinga helped to forge the Angolan identity. Today, she is a cultural icon for various groups in present-day Angola. Ambassador, negotiator, strategist and compatriot, Njinga is a key historical figure essential to understanding the construction of Angolan identity.

During the Angolan war of liberation (1961–1974), nationalist leaders revived the memory of Njinga and made her an icon of independence. In 1975, when the country's independence was proclaimed, her statue was erected in Luanda as a symbol of resistance and freedom. Today, Njinga features prominently in the popular imagination of Angola as a symbol of identity, resistance and social cohesion.

Statue of Njinga Mbandi, Luanda, Republic of Angola.

## A Pan-African symbol

The spirit of resistance and freedom symbolized by Queen Njinga has spread well beyond the borders of Angola. Today, this queen is the embodiment of a central image in African history, that of resistance to Europe's colonialist goals.

After Njinga's death, many African countries resisted and fought for centuries for independence, which they obtained at last in the twentieth century. In Africa, Njinga's memory has been an inspiration in the struggle for independence.

The figure of Njinga Mbandi in the *Congada* procession, Brazil.
© UNESCO/Luciano Osorio, 2011.

The *Congada* procession in Brazil.
© UNESCO/ Luciano Osorio, 2011.

# A reference in societies where there are people of African descent

Njinga's influence has spread as far as the Americas, where people of African descent know of her from stories, legends and the spirit of resistance that crossed the Atlantic in the slave ships. Queen Njinga is part of the collective memory of the Afro-Atlantic world.

Accordingly, many *capoeira*[1] groups have been named after her in Brazil. Rosângela Costa Araújo, also known as *Mestre Janja*, drew inspiration from the "double Queen" in establishing the Njinga Capoeira Angola Group Institute, a centre for education and social integration through *capoeira*. Its main goal is to promote gender equality within this traditionally male-dominated discipline.

---

1   *Capoeira* is an expression of Afro-Brazilian culture, a symbol of resistance that combines martial art, popular culture and music.

*Mestre Janja* in her *Capoeira* school in Brazil.

# Bibliography

The feats of the "double Queen" are recorded in a host of documents, such as Portuguese military accounts, governors' archives, Njinga's letters to the Portuguese kings João IV and Alfonso VI, and the accounts of two Italian missionaries who successively resided at her court (Antonio de Gaete and Antonio Cavazzi da Montecuccolo).

Furthermore, there is now a substantial body of Angolan, Portuguese and Brazilian scholarly literature on the Queen. Oral tradition, too, has done much to keep the memory of Queen Njinga's story alive.

Benjamin, R., Neto, J.B. and Alves, A. 2008. *A Rainha Ginga, A Africa está em nós* [Queen Ginga, Africa is within us]. Baobá Collection.

Cavazzi, A. 1687 (2010). *Njinga, Reine d'Angola. La Relation d'Antonio Cavazzi de Montecuccolo* [Njinga, Queen of Angola. As told by Antonio Cavazzi de Montecuccolo, translated by X. de Castro and A. du Cheyron d'Abzac.] Paris: Editions Chandeigne.

Kake, I.B. 1975. *Anne Zingha, Reine d'Angola* [Anne Zingha, Queen of Angola]. Paris: Editions ABC.

Lienhard, M. 2000. *Ginga, Rainha 1582-1663* [Queen Ginga 1582-1663]. Anais de História de Além-Mar [Annals of the History of the Overseas Territories]. Lisbon, No. 1, pp. 245–272.

Mata, I. (ed.). 2012. *A Rainha Nznga Mbandi: História, Memória e Mito* [Queen Nznga Mbandi, History, Memory and Myth]. Colóquio Internacional sobre a Rainha Nznga Mbandi [International Symposium on Queen Nznga Mbandi]. Lisbon.

Mussa, A. 2007. *O Trono da Rainha Jinga* [Queen Ginga's Throne]. Record. Rio de Janeiro, São Paulo.

Pacavira, M.P. 1985. *Nznga Mbandi. União dos escritores angolanos* [Union of Angolan Writers]. Luanda.

Randles, W. 1969. *L'ancien royaume du Congo, des origines à la fin du XIX$^e$ siècle* [The Ancient Kingdom of the Congo from Antiquity to the End of the Nineteenth Century]. Paris: Mouton.

Serrano, C. 1995/1996. *Ginga, a Rainha Quilombola de Matamba e Angola* [Ginga, the Quilombola Queen of Matamba and Angola]. Revista USP No. 28, Dossier Povo Negro, 300 anos [The Black People File, 300 years].

UNESCO. 1998. *General History of Africa,* Volume V. Paris: UNESCO Publishing.

# Books in the Women in African History series:

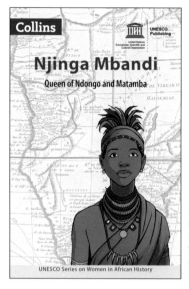

Njinga Mbandi, Queen of Ndongo and Matamba, was a deft diplomat, skilful negotiator and formidable tactician, who resisted Portugal's colonial designs tenaciously until her death in 1663.

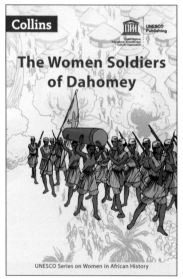

The Women Soldiers of Dahomey were elite troops who contributed to the military power of the Kingdom of Dahomey in the eighteenth and nineteenth centuries.

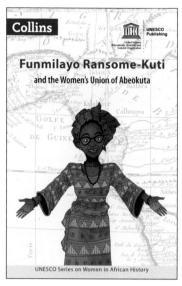

Funmilayo Ransome-Kuti founded the Abeokuta Women's Union, one of the most impressive women's organizations of the twentieth century which fought to protect and further the rights of women.

Wangari Maathai was a Kenyan environmental activist who founded the Green Belt Movement, which encourages people, particularly women, to plant trees to combat environmental degradation. She was awarded the Nobel Peace Prize in 2004.

GENERAL HISTORY OF AFRICA

For additional pedagogical resources, please visit the website:

www.unesco.org/womeninafrica

The UNESCO Project Women in African History was realized with the financial contribution of the Republic of Bulgaria.

Republic of Bulgaria